Anonymus

The Naples

Hand Guide

Anonymus

The Naples
Hand Guide

ISBN/EAN: 9783741184291

Manufactured in Europe, USA, Canada, Australia, Japa

Cover: Foto ©Lupo / pixelio.de

Manufactured and distributed by brebook publishing software
(www.brebook.com)

Anonymus

The Naples

.

THE NAPLES

HAND GUIDE

NAPLES
PRINTED BY CAVALIERE GENNARO DE ANGELIS
Portamedina alla Pignasecca, 44
1873

Adolfo Bencini

CORAL LAVA

AND

TORTOISESHELL

MANUFACTURER

Strada S. Carlo N. 28

NAPLES

PREFACE

The object of the present descriptions of Naples and its environs are to render the traveller as independant as possible ; to supply him with some informations deserving notice in visiting the places and objects the most interesting. The present little guide is divided into two parts the first for Naples, and the other for its environs. The former part we limit ourselves in few observations as to its situation history and present state of the town. As to the second we have prefered the typographical order for the different separate objects.

NAPLES

Naples is situated at 40°-51'-47" north latitude and 11°-54'-40" east of Paris. No town in Europe is better situated. It has the appearance of an Amphitheatre, above a Crater of about 73 miles in circumference from Cape Miseno, to the point of Posillipo, closed on one side by the Island of Capri, and Procida and Ischia on the other. On the north of Naples rises Vesuvius isolated ; that fully compensate our little and momentary fears by the beautiful and sublime sight of its eruption. No place will be found more populate than at the foot of the Vulcano. In sight of Naples and almost chained to each other lie the fine Villages of Portici, Resina, the two tower ôf Del Greco, and Annunziata with the remains of Erculanum and Pompei. On the other side the Posillipo hill with the tombs of Virgilio and Sannazzaro. The chain of the Appenine is alto seen at a distance, a spur of which surrounding Vesuvius it parts and joins a portion of the Naples Crater near Cape Misene. On this side and opposite Naples lies Castellamare, Vico, Sorrento where Tasso was born, and Massa. All this forms a most beautiful picturesque and theatrical appearance and reminds one to be worth visiting. The origin of Naples is lost in tradition of the greatest antiquity. It is stated that a Syren named Partenope built a town on its shore, but according to others it was built by Eumelo a leader of Fenician colony and. Father to Partenopo. (The new city) Neapolis was then the name given to the new city till the arrival of the Athenian colony, then it was naturally called by the name of old city orPalepoli, but on the joining of both cities the Name of Naples prevailed. It was then subjected to the Roman dominion. They were moderate and generous towards it-perhaps to eujoy their residence there better. After the fall of the Roman Empire Naples met with the general fate of all the Italian towns and fell under Odoacre King of the Oscans. The Goths became masters aftonwards and then the Esarchis who established themselves at Ravenna in 567. The Longobards invited in 568 by Narsate founded then a powerful kingdom in Italy, but never took possession of Naples. The Emperor of the East had sent Dukes to govern it in their name, who took the title of Consuls and dukes of Naples, fortifying themselves against the Longobards, but 3 years after,

Sergio Duke of Naples by the aid of the Normans
regained his duchy. In 1139 Naples submitted to
Roger King of Sicily as all the other town of the
Kingdom had done. King Roger came to Naples
in 1140. Here ends the private history of Naples
and joins that of Italy. An interesting part of the
history of Naples will be the ampliation it has
received in the different epocs, as far as the present time, becoming one of the principal cities in
Europe both in size and population. It is considered more than half a milion of inhabitants,
and by the purchase of one of its own king Naples
has in 1734 become the principal City in Italy.
Under King Charles of Burbon the Port was en-
largedand a new street was opened with a bridge
to the sea, and fortified, enlarged the Royal Palace, and built the Palace of Capodimonte, S.
Carlos Theatre constructed in 270 days, built the
Royal Poor house (Albergo de'Poveri) the Cavalry
barruchs built, and the Seraglio for wild beasts.
These comodities have been continued by Ferdinand the son of Charles viz, the Mergelline street,
Posillipo, the Camp, Capodimonte street, Chiaia,
the warehouses at the Ponte Maddalena, the palace square the illumination of the town. Botanic Garden, the Museum, Academy, Observa-
tory, Military College, several schools ec. The
reign of the Burbons was interrupted in 1799 by
the Republic and Monarchy of Joseph Buona-
parte and Gioachin Murat from 1806 to 1815. In
the month of may 1860 Joseph Garibaldi landed
at Marsala in Sicily with 1000 men, took possession of the Island which was in a revolutionary
state against the Bourbons, crossed Calabria and
entered Naples on the 7 of september 1860. He
was joyfully received by the Neapolitans, who

being left masters of their own fate by the *Plebiscito* of the 21 october 1860 joined the rest of the Italian Peninsula under the scepter of Vittorio Emmanuel the Second.

ARRIVAL IN NAPLES

On arriving in Naples either by sea or land the traveller is subjected to a Custom house visit-here he will find the tarif.

BOATS

Travellers coming prom foreign places, north Italy or Sicily with luggage or without .   L.   1 00
From Salerno, or Gaeta . . . . . »   40
From the islands of Capri Ischia Pro-) »   20
cida or any place in the bay of Naples.)

LUGGAGE

From mole to the carriage 1 single
trunk non exceeding 100 kilos . . . . »   50
From 100 to 200 kilos . . . . . . »   60
From the entrance, or station and vi-
ceversa one single trunk of 100 kilos . . »   20
From 101, to 200 kilos . . . . . . »   40
Small luggage, bags, hat boxes, purse »   20
One trunk from the Post or Station to
the Hotel 100 kilos . . . . »   1 00
From 101 to 200 kilos . . . . . . »   1 50
In case of any dispute with the boatmen or coachmen, it would be prudent to take the number and apply to the Questura Piazza del Municipio, or to any of the Municipal guards or Police, whece one may obtain redress.

TOWN CARRIAGES
From day break to Midnight

One horse carriage	*Two horse carriage*
The fare. . . L. 0,60	The fare. . . L. 1,20
By the hour. 1 hour 1,40	By the hour. 1 hour 2,10
The following hours 1,00	The following hours 1,50

From midnight to day break

The fare . . . L. 1,00	The fare . . L. 1,00
By the hour. 1 hour 2,00	By the hour. 1 hour 3,00
The following hours 1,40	The following hours 2,00

FARES OF CARRIAGES OUT OF TOWN

From Naples to Po-silipo . L. 1,50	From Naples to Po-sillipo . L. 2,25
» » to Capodi-monte . » » Arenella or ⎱ 1,30 » » Antignano ⎰ » » Vomero .	» » to Capodi-monte . » » ArenellaAn-⎱ 2,25 tignano . ⎰ » » Vomero .
» » Fuori Grotta 1,20	» » Fuorigrotta. 1,75
» » Bagnoli Lago di Agnano . 2,00	» » Bagnoli Lago Agnano . 3,00
» » Piscinola. . 2,50	» » Miano e Ma-rianella . . 3,00
» » Portici. . . 1,75	» » Piscinola. . 3,75
» » S. Giorgio a Cremano . 1,75	» » Portici . . 2,50
» » Darra . . . 1,75	» » S. Giorgio a Cremano. . 2,50
» » Resina. . . 2,00	» » Barra . . . 2,50
» » Tor.delGreco 2,50	» » Resina. . . 3,00
	» » Tor.delGreco 3,75

P.S. To the above prices a little addition is al-
ways allowed to Coachmen, when taken to a place
further than the place stated by the traveller or
from that he wished to go. The traveller kas a right

to the carriage of his small baggage for every
trunk 20 centimes extra.

POST OFFICES

General Post Office, Strada Monteoliveto.

(Snccursales), Piazza S. Caterina a Chiaia.
    id.   Strada Foria n. 147.
    id.   Railway Station.
    id.   Immaculatella, close to the Port

TELEGRAPHS

Central Office, Strada Monteoliveto.

(Succursale), Strada S. Teresa a Chiaia.
    id.   Strada S. Giacomo n. 42.
    id.   Strada Foria n. 108.

VALERY BROTHERS and SON

French line of Steam Packet Office

Every Wednesday and Friday

FOR

MARSEILLE

calling at CIVITAVECCHIA LEGHORN and GENOA

Meeting the Steamer for

Cette, Nice, Grasse, Cannes, Porto Torres etc.

For freight ec. apply

to Mess.rs L. BALSAMO et C.°

Strada Piliero N. 1.

NAPLES

I. and **V. FLORIO** et C.

Steam Packet Office

for PALERMO

EVERY

Monday, Wednesday, Thursday, Friday and Saturday

At **6** p. m.

On Friday — A steamer will leave *Palermo* for Leghorn and Genoa

On Saturday will leave *Palermo* for Messina Catania, Siracusa and Malta.

For freight apply at N. 30 Strada Piliero

NAPLES

CONSULAR AGENTS

France, Via Poerio n. 34.
England, Vico Calascione Pizzofalcone.
Autria, Strada S. Giacomo n. 29.
Russia, Via Poerio n. 34.
Germany, Fontana Medina n. 47.
Spain, Palazzo Ciccarelli S. Maria degli Angioli.
Belgium, Strada Donnalbina n. 56.
Holland, Piazza del Muicipio n 52.
Principality of Monaco, Strada della Pace.
Denmark, Vico primo Piliero n. 1.
Republic of S. Marino, Vico Carogiojello n. 15.
Portugal Toledo n. 329.
Greece, Via Poerio n. 34.
Turkey, Riviera di Chiaia n. 48.
United States of America, Piazza del Municipio n. 52.
Colombia, Strada dei Pellegrini n. 19.
New Granada, Porta Medina n. 49.
Republic of Guatimale, Largo Mondragone n. 3.
Repnblicof Salvador. Toledo n. 185.
Republic Argentina, Piazza del Municipio n. 52.
Brasile, Toledo n. 424.
Bolivia strada Costantinopoli n. 30.
Perù, Pizzo Falcone n. 73.
Chili, Strada S. Giacomo n. 29.
Costa Ricca, Fontana Medina n. 5.
Equador, Strada S. Pasquale a Chiaja n. 19.
Messico, Porta Medina n. 49.
Repubblic di Uraguay, Via Gennaro Serra 69.
Persia, Piazza del Municipio n. 8.
Republic of Honduras, Strada Pace n. 27.

CENTRAL POLICE OFFICE

Strada Concezione, Toledo.

PROTESTANT CHURCHES

German and French, Via Carlo Poerio.
Scotch, Strada S. Maria a Cappella

12

English Strada S. Pasquale a Chiaia.
Weslyan Chapel. Toledo n. 210.
Valdese, Magno Cavallo n. 80.
Synagoge, Vico Cappella Vecchia a Chiaia.
A nen Turch now building, Vico sargente Maggio-
re Toledo.

THATRES AND CLUBS

Teatro San Carlos. Neac the Royal Palace.
Teatro del Fondo, Strada del Molo.
Teatro Fiorentini, Strada Fiorentini.
Teatro National, Vico Lungo Teatro Nuovo.
Teatro Fenice, Piazza del Municipio.
Rossini, Salita Tarsia.
S. Carlino, Piazza del Municipio.
Giardino d'Inverno, Villa Nazionale.
Politeama, Strada Monte di Dio.
S. Ferdinando, Strada Ponte Nuovo. Foria.
Teatro Partenope, Piazza Cavour.
Teatro Goldoni, Strada S. Tommaso d'Aquino.
Bellini, Fosse del Grano.
National Club, Largo Vittoria.
Casino dell'Unione, San Carlos Theatre.
Cerchio dell'Accademia, Piazza S. Ferdinando.

Royal Palace Naples, Built in 1600 by the Architect Domenico Fontana, il contains large and richly
dceorated apartments, a Chapel ornamented with
fine marbles ûnd pictures. The magnificent Stair
case with its statues of Ebro and Jago was constructed in 1651. The saloon contains several modern pictures. In the first antichamber there is the
Holy Family a fine picture by Spagnoletto. On
the side facing the square a small theatre, and a
splendid dining room. The state room is richly ornamented with fine red velvet and gildings. The
broidering was made by the working people at the
Poor house in 1818. The *bas relief* rep resent the different provinces of the Kingdom. It follows a fine

gallery with very fine Sevre vases, and a beautiful
Writing desk a gift from the town of Naples. In
another apartment Leonardo da Vinci, presenting.
the last supper to the donor by Podesti. In another room the Portrait of Van Dyrk and several
others, of great merit.

By enquiring from the Porter at the gate of the
Palace the traveller will be shown to the office of
the superintendant of the Palace where tickets for
admitting six persons will be given gratis, and
which will also be valid to admit them to the Palace of Capodimonte, Caserta, Favorita, Quisisana
the Astroni garden. The ticket must be shewn to
the Porter at each of these places.

Royal Palace of Capodimonte, Situated in the most
beautiful and elevated spot of Naples was begun
by Charles the third in 1738 and finished by Ferdinand 2.^{d} in 1834 with fine gardens and a beautiful
View. The apartments are shewn where there is a
collection of picture of the Neapolitan school, two
picture One of Camerucci the death of Caesar et Vir-
ginia, aud the other by Benvenuto. Giudith. Each
room has a catalogue of the picture. The first has a
collection of ancient arms among them the helmet
and shield of Roger, the sword which Louis 14°,
gave to Philip of Anjoù. The arms of Alexander
Farnese. Victor Amedeo of Savoj. One of the room
is made of China manufactured at Capodimonte,
which has now become very rare. The park is very
pretty and strangers will be pleased to take a turn
in it.

Royal Palace of Caserta, The fine and healthy spot
induced Ring Charles of Burbon to build this Palace and on the 20 January 1752, the first founda-
tion stone was laid with great pomp and solemni-
ty. The building was carried on with great activity
by the celebrated Architect Vunvitelli, so that in
1759 when Charles came to hold the Spanish Monarchy it had already reached the upper floor. It

was after accomplished by his son Ferdinand. To
have an idea of its immense size, one must cast a
glance froim its centre and then look at its great
stair case of 117 marble steps all of one piece each.
On the first floor a chapel ornamented with fine
marbles, lapis lazuli, and gildings. The theatre after supported by 16 pilars brought from the Temple of Serapide near Puzzuoli. It is considered one
of the greatest and magnific Palaces it is 35 metres
in height and about 200 wide. It has 240 windows
in front. In continuation of the Palace a beautiful
park and gardens with fountains. The bason and
Water fall lie opposite its immense front, and are
about 2 Kilometres distant from the Palace gate.
The water are carried by a long way crossing from
Maddaloni through an aqueduct with three rows of
arches called the Ponte della Valle. A permit to
visit these places in a carriage would be necessary
in order to render the excursion more pleasant.

Palace of S. Giacomo. A colossal building, it was
began in 1819 aud finished in 1825. It has four large entrances. It is the residence of the Municipality. Questura and their offices, and several others.
That of the Prefecture is situated in Piazza del Plebiscito. Palazzo della Foresteria.

National Museum, Situated at the further end of
Toledo on an elevated point, was built in 1587. The
most remarkable objects, beside the Gallery of Paintings, are those found in Pompei and Erculanum
sculptures, bas relief-bronz, mosaic, frescos, ornaments, terracotta, hardstone, greek roman and
etruscan works. Open every day from 9 to 3 p. m.
entrance one frank Sunday gratis open from 10 to
4 p. m. The catalogue of all the object existing in
the National Museum is to be had at the exhibition
hall on the ground floor.

National Villa, Or public walk is situated at the
Riviera di Chiaia, it is 4500 feet long by 200 wide.
The first half was made in 1780, it is divided into

five valleys. A fine fountain in the middle with a
large entire granite basin found amongst the anti-
quities of Paestum, it was first taken to Salerno,
and from there to Naples. Four more side fountains with statues, terraces, flowers, benches, coffè
houses The second half was added in 1807, and
offers a beautiful wood and walks, and a terrace
over the sea, two small temples one to Virgil, and
the other to Tasso, and several other ornaments.
An other portion was added in 1834 of 1500 feet
long. On the right it is sided by the Riviera di
Chiaia, a fashionable drive in the afternoon, and on
the left by a new street now constructing, which
from S. Lucia leads to Mergellina coasting the sea,
and which is considered the finest and most pleasant that Naples can offer coasting the sea on one
side, and Palaces and the Villa on the other. At the
farther end of the Villa before entering the street of
Piedigrotta on the right the new road Corso Vittorio Emmannele, a beautiful place has now become
very populate for the quantity of houses and Palaces built, and it runs as far as the Infrascata close
to the National Museum. It offers one of the finest
views, forming the entire Panorama of the town
below.

The Zoological station. Is situated in the centre of
the Garden–This imposing edifice has been erected
to furnish the scientific world with a great zoological laboratory, intended especially to facilitate the
study of marine animals with which the bay of Naples abounds. The lower part of the building is occupied by a great Aquarium, the dimensions of
which are superior to those of the similar institutions of Berlin, Hamburgh, and the crystal palace
Sydenham That of Brighton is larger but it cannot
be compared with the Naples aquarium for the mul-
titude and variety of the animals exhibited in the
tanks. In this respect indeed the latter must al-
ways remain unrivalled on account of its favou-
rable position on the sea shore and the richness of

the fauna of this part of the mediterranean. The aquarium is open to the pubblic from eight ò clock in the morning to six in the evening, on the payment of 2 franks during the winter months (from October to May) and one franck for the rest of the year. The upper story is occupied by the laboratories, the library, and the apartments for the naturalists who direct the establishment. The laboratories contain twenty tables, the greater part of which have been taken by the different Governments of Europe who send their Naturalists here for the purpose of studying.

The founder and director of the establishment is a youny German naturalist D.r Anton Dohrn. He erected the building at his own expense, assisted by a subvention from the German Empire. The Municipality of Naples gratuitously ceded the site. in returu for which the propriety right of the whole establishment will revert to the city of Naples after thirty years.

The revenues of the institutions are entirely devoted to the furtherance of zoological studies in every possible mammer. This is the first establishment of the kind.

Piazza de' Martiri. Anciently called Largo Cappella Vecchia, was to be called Piazza della Pace, but was afterward fixed to the present one, offers a new monument erected to the Martyrs of the Italian Liberty. The granite pillar of one single piece, and which supports the statue of Victory cast by Cav. Caggiani was the gift of the Emperor of Russia to Ferdinand the 2° of Burbon. The building was directed by the Architect Albino, and the four Lions shewing ihe different period undergone by Italy-viz-the revolutions of 1799-1820-1818-1860-were made by concurrency from the Neopolitan Artists Soluri-Ricca Lista and Ruscolino.

Grotta di Pozzuoll. Or blue grotto — It extends about half a milo dug in the rock a Colossal work

of the ancient Roman-lighted with gas night and
day. There are steps at its entrance leading to the
tomb of Virgil. to be seen by half a frank to the
Guardian.

Botanic Garden. Situated in the fine street of Foria, depending from the University. Its date is 1809-
beside a rich collection of all kind of plants has
four erb gardens. Autographs of the most celebrated Botanists-tools, and a library.

Catacombs. At S. Gennaro dei poveri, contain
subterrancon diggings in the rock in the shape of
corridors, rooms and rotondas and have mostly
three stores communicating to each other by steps
The principal corridors are about 20 feet in height
and au unequal width. The walls have niches, five
or six of them are one above the other. They were covered with marble and inscriptions. which
have been barbarously cut to pave the church of
S. January, where are still seen-and also for other
purpose. Most of the inscriptions belong to Chri-
stians, none have been found belongig to Pagans to
find out their epoc. They extend for several miles in
endless branches.

Burying ground. (Camposanto) Situated at Poggio
reale preferible to any for its rare peculiarities and
fine monuments, it loads from Foria street and de-
serves to be seen.

Protestant buryinq ground. Out of Porta Capuana
very pretty built. A quantity of English, Germans
Russians and American names are seen.

Poorhouse. (Albergo dei poveri) in the Foria street
a large and vast building, constructed by Charles
3° in 1751, it has a church inside and four convents
5000 poor are lodged there both male and female
employed in different trades. There also 60 more
Asylum for the poor in Naples, and several have
rich dowry.

2

Castle Ovo. Erected in 1154, called after its oval shape joins the land at S. Lucia and Chiatamone.

Castle Capuano· Dates from 1231. An ancient residence of Vice-kings. In 1546 Peter of Toledo reduced it to the shape of a Palace, and collected in it all the Tribunals which were about the town as they are at present.

Castle Nuovo. Built in 1283 by Charles the first of Anjou, it was the residence of the king of that family. the Aragones, and spanish Vice-king.
Alfonso I. of Aragon enlarged it by adding the towers. Peter of Toledo built the walls, and Charles 3. of Burbon gave its present shape. The beautipul triumphal arch, the bronze gates on which the victories of Ferdinand I. against the rebel Barons and John of Anjou are figured (made by Jo Monaco) are valued to several milions of franks. The arch was made to celebrate the entrance of king Alphonso I.

Castle S. Erme. It commands the whole town and it is placed on the most elevated point. Its origin is lost in tradition. There was formerly a tower named Belforte, which was changed into a Castle by Charles II in 1518. Naples being at that time besieged by General Lautree its fortifications were encreased, and by order of Charles V, became in 1535 a regular citadel. Some other additions were also made by Philip 5, There is a large square in the centre of this castle for practising, and a large cistern beneath it dug in the rock, of an enormous size-viz, as wide as the Castle.

Castle of Carmine. In 1647 Masaniello with his revolutions gave origin to its fortification.

CHURCHES

The number of Churches in Naples rivals with that of Rome, there are more than 350, each of them might be called a Museum for the richness of their mouuments and pictures, and it would require many volumes to give a full description of them we therefore cite some of the principal.

The Cathedral (Duomo) It dates from 1299 and is one of the largest and most ancient that Naples can boast of. There were anciently in its place two temples one to Apollos, and the other to Neptune. It was built by Charles 1 of Anjou, and finished by Charles the 2. Having fallen down in 1456 by an earthquake, it was repaired by Alfonso 1, by the support of several noble families, the coat of arms of which were engraved on the pillars. This large church contains valuable monuments. Over the large door the tombs of Charles I, and his wife Clemenza are seen. The font on the left is formed of a large ancient vase of Egyptian Casalta, held by a porfid pedestal; it was one time consacrated to Baccus. The sacristy rich with valuable furniture, contains also several portraits of Neapolitan Archbishops and their tombs. Near the sacristy door the tomb of Andrew, the husband of Johanna 1, strangled at Aversa. The S. January chapel, called the Treasure, is very richly furnished with silver statues, furniture, and sacred vases of great value and paintings by clever artists. The chapel alone is valued five milions of franks The blood of s. January is deposited in it, the liquifation of which happens three times a year.

St. Martin Cortosa. Placed under the castle S. Ermo was founded by Charles the son of Robert of Anjeù in 1400 contains several frescos by Miccio Spadaro, and Bellisario, and some pictures by Spagnoletto Guido Reni, and Stanzione, on the left of the altar another by Spagnoletto representing the Communione of the Apostles by Christ, and saveral more of great merit. The situation of this magnific building, is one of the finest ever seen, and to enjoy it the more it is necessary entering the garden, and particulary the Belvedere. To the singular beauties of nature it adds a great many prices of art, Nothing can be compared to the richness of the church the fine ornaments of which are joined to taste. A museum has lately been formed there by care of Commendatore Fiorelli Director of the National Museum, which adds much interest to this church, and which may be classified among the first in Italy.

- **Chapel of S. Severo.** Built in 1613 by Alexander di Sangro, for the purpose of forming a burial place for the famijy of Sangro Prince of St. Severo. It is covered with a profusion of marbles and frescos-by Corenzio, Solimene and Giordano. Among the different statues the one by Quiroli is most remarkable in its Kind, forming a man wrapped in a net. Anotherby Corradini representing Chastity wrapped in a veil through which the features of the body are distinctly seen; and the last superior to any for its perfection made by Napoletano Sammartino in 2751 representing a dead Christ laid on a base covered with a veil, through which the anatomical parts of the body are distinctly seen.

The Carmine. Where Massaniello is buried, and the monuments of Corradino of Sweden, and Frederich of Austria both executed by order of Charles of Anjoù in the Marhet place in 1268.

S. Domenico Maggiore. Built in 1289.

Santa Chiara. Built in 1310 by King Robert of Anjoù. The different tombs of the Neapolitan Kings are to be seen. Behind the altar a monument erected to the same King Robert drawn by Masuccio the first. It was greatly embellished in 1744 and enriched with several drawings by Giotto, and Cavaliere Conca. On the left of the altar there is a Chapel forthe Princes of the house of Burbons.

Ss. Apostoll It dates from the 17 century.

St. Gacomo del Spagnoll. Built in 1540 among its

monuments, there is that of Peter of Toledo, one of the finest work of Giovanni Merliano.

The Annunziata. Erected by Sancia the wife of Robert, and enlarged by Iohanna 2. A fire on the night of 8. February 1757 destroyed it, but il was repaired and bronght to an end in 1782. The archited was Vanvitelli. Some fine frescos are to be seen Attached to the church there is a house, the chief purpose of which is to recover foundlings.

S. Giovanni Maggiore. The moxt ancient church.

S. Giovanni a Carbonara. Il dates from 1400.

S. Pietro a Majella. Built in the time of Alfonso 2.^{d} by Pipino. There are some fine pictures. The Music College is now in the old Monastèry. There is also a valuable library, the produce of the moxt celebrated master and some autographs. The Commendatore Lauro Rossi has now the direction of the College.

Gerolomini. Built in 1700.

S. Maria la Nuova. Built in 1599.

S. Francis di Paola. A modern building in 1817, after the plan of Bianchi di Lugano, it is situated opposite the Royal Palace. Its architecture is an imitation of the Panteon at Rome; The eight colossal statues in the interior of the church represent the four Evangelists, and as many Doctors of the church, and are made by Carrara artists, and S. Mark by a Venitian. The Cupola offers a fine view, and fine step to get to it.

The Gesù Nuovo. Built in 1584, very rich of marbles. The entrance door is finely worked. The church is ornamented with frescos by Solimene, Corenzio. Stanzioni and Vaccaro. The cupola is by Laufrancs. There are other paintings by Giordano, Battistello. Spagnoletto, Siciliani, and other. The altar is richly furnished with Agath and jaspar. Before this church there is an Obeliske erected by a Gesuit in 1747. It is noticeable.

The University. Contains 25000 volumes open from 9 to 3 p. m.

Libreria Nazionale. At the National Museum.

Libreria Brancacolana. At S. Angelo a Nilo, it conains 70000 volumes, and 7000, ms.

Libreria S. Giacomo. Strada Concezione Toledo.

Librar y of Cerolomini. Opposito the Cathedral.

The Grandi Archives. In the convent of. S. Severino and Sossia the University.

Royal Academy of Archeology. Literature and fine arts.

Pontanian Academy.

Istituto d'Incoraggiamento, oi Tecnical Schools Salita Tarsia.

Istituto di Fine arts.

HOSPITALS

Hospital Pace.

Hospital Pellegrini.

Asylum of S. Joseph et Luca.
Annunziata. Foundling hospital.

Clinical Hospital of Gesù e Maria.

English Hospital, at the Marine Hospital strada Picdigrotta.

Hospital degli Inourabili. Strada Foria. This large Hospital divided into 43 rooms contains 1300 sick persons. An Ostretic Room with 50 beds. Private boarding and lodging rooms. There are several cle-

ver and able Doctors and Surgeons, among them
D. Vincenzo Martone, who for his skill and honest
proceeding is generally employed by travellers. He
lives n.° 21. Salita Trinità degli Spagnoli. Naples.

ENVIRONS OF NAPLES

Camaldoli. Situated on the highest hill round Naples, from which the most splendid view can bo
seen; is one of the best excursions and the easiest
one. Donkeys can be hired for about fr. 1,50. Very
little is to be seen both in the Church and Convent
only the view of the bays of Naples Pozzuoli and
Gaeta.

Pozzuoli, Baia, Cuma. To visit these places we pass
through the Grotto of Puzzuoli. The village out the
grotta is called *Fuori Grotta* where the tomb of the
philologist and poet Giacomo Leopardi is to be seen
beneath the vestibule of the little church of S. Vi-
tale. Stopping in the centre we find on the right
the Camaldoli, and on the left the hill of Posilipo,
and opposite a road leading to the sea. Two roads
follow after , one leading to Puzzuoli, and the
other to the lake of Agnano. On visiting the latter
place, and without losing much of the way, we find
on arriving the baths of St. January, a name deri-
ved from the Bishop of Capua of that name, when
he bathed there. Higher one finds the *Grotto del Ca-
ne* then that of the *Amoniac.* Following the same direction one reaches the *Monti Leucogù* or *Monti Bianchi*, at the foot of which one finds the mineral spring
of *Pisciarelli*, good for any skin disease. After lea-
ving this lake one reaches the road to Pozzuoli,
and which offers a beautiful view of the Island of
Nisida on the left with its ancient port, and on the
right the *Campi Fleqreni*. On the south Pozzuoli, Ca-
po Miseno, Monte Nuovo, Baia, the Campi di Averno and Eliseo, and further on the island of Procida, and at last the Gigantic Island of Capri. This
place called Bagnoli abounds with, termo mineral

waters, and supplied with several bathing esta-
blishments. On crossiny the side of a Rocky ill formed of vulcanic materials one reaches Pozzuoli anciently the Emporium of Cuma, and Campania Felice. Next to it there is the *Solfatara*. A Crater of
half estinguished vulcano. the ground beneath is
empty, and it sounds by throwing a stone. Further
down lies the *Amphitheatre*, larger than that of Pompei and Verona, but not so vast as those of Rome
or Capua, containing no more than 35000 persons.
It was in this amphitheatre that St. January and
other Martyrs were left to be eaten by wild beasts.
At a short distance there is the Theatre in an oval
shape, ruins of the aucient Ferma called The temple of Diana, and Neptune. The villa of Cicero and
the temple of Serapide were discovered in 1759. The
pillars which held the Cupola were taken to the Royal Palace of Caserta, and the statues and vases
to the National Museum. It is one of the most interesting building of Pozzuoli, being remarkable
both for the richness of its marbles, and artistical
taste, in its construction. It is said to have been
dedicated to Jupiter and at the same time a Pan-
theon and Thermae. Crossing the road leading to
Baia we see *Monte Nuovo* it dates 30 September 1838.
An eruption which lasted 48 hours dertroyed the
village called Pergole and raised this hill in its
place.

Lake Lucrino, to the west of Mount Nuovo was
partly destroyed by the same eruption and close
by it the.

Lago di Averno, from which Virgil makes Eneas
descend into hell. Agrippa desiring to give a new
port to the Roman fleet made these two lakes com-
municate by means of a canal at which milions of
slaves were employed, but the same eruption which created Mount Nuovo effaced every trace of their
labour.

The Grotta della Sibilla, With baths of the same

name, and others larger, mark the Temple of Apollo, and Mercury, offers no interest whatever. From the lake d'Averno going northbwards we gain the highway leading to.

Arco felice di Cuma, This town which was situaled on a hill close to the sea has a speciality in history on account of its glories and misfortunes. It is the most ancient Grecian colony and.

Arco felice, was its principal entrance. A colossal trunk of the statue of Iupiter was found in the so called.

Temple of the Plants, Other ruins as temples, fortress, walls cc. are spread about this country.

The Lake Fusaro, Anciently called *Acherusia* was famous for its oysters. Ruins villas and tombs are still to be seen on its banks, and a canal constructed by the Romans leading to the sea. From Fusaro you go to Miseno passing through Baja a summer place for the Romans then Bacoli whare Nero received his mother pretending to be reconciled to her in order to better dissemble the odious plan he had made against her life.

The Cento Camerelle, or Labyrinth or prisons of Nero, are in all probability the cellars of one of his villas.

The Piscina Mirabile, A vast reservoir of Water for the use of the fleet and private persons, 48 pillars support the roof. With a large aqueduct Claudio joined this reservoir, taking the waters from the province of Avellino about 100 Kilometre distance.

Lago Miseno rising to a peak above the sea ; it took its name from a trumpeter of Eneas, who according to Virgil was buried there. Augustus made a port called by the same name in order to give refuge to the Roman fleet in the Mediterranean. It had three basins, the principal of which.

Mare morto, a crater of an ancient Vulcano. Between Cape Miseno and Mount Procida is

Millscola where the soldiers manoeuvred. Several inscriptions found there tell us the name of those soldiers aud sailors who carried off the prizes.

From Cape Miseno yon can almost touch the two islands of Ischia and Procida so near are they to the continent; they are originally volcanic,and once formed only one. They aboundwith thermo mineral waters , and are a charming villeggiatura in summer. A regular service of steamboats between Naples and the islands is an attraction to visitors being able to go forwards and backwards twice a day. From the Epomeo, or (Mount St. Nicolas) is seen a beautiful view of the three gulfs of Gaeta, Naples, and Salerno.

Baja, The temples of Diana, Venus and Mercury, or Truglio, the Baths of Iritoli (hot mineral water) and the stoves of Nero which are supposed to have communicated with these baths. From Baja one returus to Naples through the town of Pozzuoli one can see the pillars of the Bridge of Caligola. The Cathedral situated on a height looking the town occupies the site of a temple of Augustus of which the colums ornamenting the church formed a part. In the interior is the tomb of Pergolesi. Arrived at Bagnoli , instead of turning to the left you may drive towards the hill coasting the sea. The building on the right contains an important chemical manufactury. Half way up is the Grotto of Sejano made by Locullus to have a direct communication between his villa aud the island of Nisida On the other side are to be seen the ruins of the Villa of Lucullus or Pollio. After passing the barrier at the turning of the street is the Church of St. Maria del Porto where is the tomb of the Poet Sannazzaro. Although we have treated this excursion so that one would think it might be done in one day, we advice travellers to divide it into two, devoting the first day to the more important part, that is Pozzuoli, Baja, Cuma, and the second to Agnano and Posillipo. Provisions are necessary to carry after.

Portici, About 4 miles distance from Naples, a fashionable Villeggiatura in summer. A royal Palace and gardens are to be seen. It dates from 1738.

Resina, The Villa Favorita of Prince of Salerno. From this place one ascend Vesuvius.

Ercolano, Not much different from Pompei there is still much buried under the lava. Several statues have heen carried to the National Museum, the finest are those of Nonio Balbo and his son. Many papyrus discovered have given the place a great importance. The remains of food, bread, eggs, fruits vegetable ec can also be seen at the Museum. The greater part of the town is still buried under the lava and scoria and the most interesting buildings discovered are those of the Theatre the Basilica, and the two houses of Argus and Aristides.

Sorrento, Native place of Torquato Tasso, fine climate, surrounded by mountains. It takes 3 hours to go up the Deserto, where a full view of the town as well as the two gulfs of Naples and Salerno can be obtained. It is famous for its manufactures of wood and musaic; several manufacturers have obtained the prize of the London and Paris exhibitions.

Castellammare, Famous for its mineral waters it is frequented by several foreigners, finely situated and is the way to Quisisana, where a Royal Palace is to be seen.

Vesuvius, Though the ascension to Vesuvius is considered fatiguing, still it becomes impossible to foreigners, to omitt it. In order therefore to avoid danger one must trust to the guide, and keep distant from the Crater as much as he possibly can. Provisions are also necessary to take with,

those found at Resina, or on the mountain are ex-
ceedingly dear. To get there the best way is to go
from Naples to Resina where guides are to be had.

Island of Capri, Famous for its wine. One can get
there by boat, or steamer to visit the.

Grotta Azzurra, Its blue waters, which being
stirred or any object in them has a beautiful silver
appearance. It was discovered in 1822, and is 53
metres long and 32 broad. The entrance is very
small and difficult, and sometimes dangerous on
account of the East and North winds.

POMPEI

Pompei is mentioned in history for the first time
in B. C. 310, but its monuments, such as the wall
of the town and the so called Greek Temple, clear-
ly prove it to be of much greater antiquity, founded by the Oscans, it soon became imbered with the
elements of Greek civilisation, like the other towns
of this extensive tribe. Being situated near the sea
on an ancient volcanic eminence, it carried on extensive commerce with the inland Campanian towns
by means of the navigable river Sarnus and enjo-
yed an uninterrupted, though not brilliant share of
prosperity. (The sea and river were separated from
the town by subsequent convulsions of nature.)
After the Samnite wars, in which Pompeii had also
partecipated, the town became subject to Rome. It
united with the other Italians in the Social war. The
rebels were *defeadet* in the vicinity of Pompeii by
Sulla, who attacked the town itself, but *unsuccess-
fully*. After the termination of the war, however,
B. C. 82, a colony of Roman soldiers was sent thither, and the inhabitants were compelled to cede
to it one, third of thier arable land. In course of
time Pompeii became thoroughly Romanised, and
was a favourite retreat of Romans of the wealthier
classes, who (c. g. Cicero) purchased estates in the

vicinity. It was also favoured by the emperors. Tacitus records a serious conflict which took place in the amphitheatre, A. D. 59, between the Pompeians and the neigbouring Nucerines, in consequence of which the former were prohibited from performing theatrical pieces for a period of 10 years. A few years later, A. D. 63, a fearful earthquake occurred, manifesting the re-awakened activity of Vesuvius, which had been quiescent for centuries. The greater part of Pompeii, its temples, colonnades, theatres, and private houses were ruined on that occasion, and the Roman senate even contemplated prohibitig its reconstruction.. Permission, however, having been granted, the town was reerected in a style more comfortable to the improved architecture of imperial Rome. The new town had not long been completed although the liberality of private persons had contributed to restore it in a remarkable short period, when il was overtaken by the catastrophe of Aug. 24th. 79. The first premonitory sympton was a dense shower of ashes, which covered the town with a stratum, about 3 fl. in depth, and allowed the inhabitants time to escape. Many of them however, returned, Some doubtless to rescue their valuables, others paralysed with fear and uncertain what course to pursue. The number of the skeletons of those who thus perished in one third part of the town already excavated is variously stated from 400 to 600. The ashes were followed by a stupendous shower of red hot rapilli, or fragments of pumice stone of all sizes, which covered the town to a depth of 7-8 ft. , and was succeded by fresh showers of ashes and again by rapilli. The present superincumbent mass is about 20 ft. in thickness. A portion of this was formed by subsequent eruptions, but the town had already been completely buried by the original catastrophe and entirely lost to view. A small village, which sprang up on or near the site, long served to maintain the name. In ancient times excavations were made, owing to which many valuable relics are probably lost to us-

but during the middle ages Pompeii was entirely
consigned to oblivion. In 1592 the architet Fontana
constructed a subterranean water conduit in order
to supply Torre dell'Annunziata from the Sarno,
actually intersecting the ruins, and to this day in
use: yet no farther investigations were then attem-
pted. In 1748 the discovery of statues and bronze
utensils by a peasant attracted the attention of
Charles III, who caused excavation to be made. The
amphitheatre, theatre, and other parts were then
disinterred. The enthusiasm called forth by the discovery has been the frequent theme of poetical
and other compositions by such celebrated authors
as Bulwer, Schiller, etc·

Under the Bourbons the ex cavation were continued in a very unsatisfactory manner. Statues and
valuables alone were extricated, whilst the ruins
were either suffered to fall to decay or covered up
again, To the reign of Murat, however, we are in-
debted for the excavation of the Forum, the town,
walls, the Street of Tombs, and many private houses. The political changes of 1860 have likervise
exercised a beneficial effect. The government has
assigned 60.000 fr. annually for the prosecution of
excavations. Under the able superintendence of M.
Fiorelli, instead of the former predatory operations
a regular plan has been adopted, according to which
the ruins are systematically explored and carefully
preserved, thus producing highly satisfactory re-
sults. A local museum and library have been insti-
tuted, a dwelling, house erected for students supported by government, and a railway constructed
for the removal of the débris. The work is prose-
cuted chiefly in the winter months, and occasio-
nally occupies several hundred labourers.

La Cava. An ancient Tyrrenian town. The Bene-
dectine Convent situated on the hill, founded on
the 11th century contains several archives of a great
importance their catalogue comprehends 8 volumes. Among these documents are the Codes of *Le-*

gum Lombardorum of 1004 and the *Volgata Latina* of
the 7th century, besides a larger number of valuable parchments and manuscripts. The church also
contains many remarkable tombs among which
those of the Abbot St. Alferius. Queen Sybilla, and
Gregory 8th. The organ is considered as one of the
best in Italy. The situation of the town calls the
attentions both of foreigners and natives, and is
much frequented as a summer residence.

AMALFI

Amalfi, a small town situated at the entrance of
a deep ravine, and surrounding by imposing, mountains and rocks of the most picturesque form,
was an import sea-port in the early part of the middle ages, rivalling Pisa and Genoa.

Amalfi, which had once contained 50,000 inhabitants, now steadly declined, and at the present day
has a population of 6506 only, who are principally
engaged in the manufacture of paper , soap and
maccaroni. The town claims to be the birthplace of
a certain Flavio Gioja, who is alleged to have invented the compass in 1302 but the story is very
doubtful. The road from Salerno, or coming from
Naples, Victri to Amalfi is much frequented, and
was completed in 1852; it is a most remarkable and
magnificent rocky route, hewn in the cliffs of the
coast, frequently supported by galleries and vast
viaducts 100 - 150 fr. above the sea level, passing
through thriving villages, and affording a succession of charming landscape. The slopes are generally somewhat bare, but are in many places laid
out in terraces and planted with, vines, olives, lemons, and fruit trees.The promontories of the coast
are occupied by massive square watch-towers, erected under Charles V as a protection against pirates, now converted into dwelling. This route is of
superior attraction to that from Castellammare to

Sorrento. The Cattedrale of S. Andrea approached prom the piazza by a broad flight of stone steps, is still, in spite of modern alterations, a remarkably interesting structure of the 11ᵗᵉ century, in the normal style. A. spacious vestibule in front, resting on 7 antique colums from Paestum, having become insecure was removed in 1865. The bronze doors, said to have been executed by Byzantine master bear two inscriptions in silver letters. The Capuchin Monastery founded in 1212 by Cardinal Pietro Capuano for monks of the Cistercian order, and built into a hollow of the rock 400 f. above the sea. It is situated about 1|2 m. to the W. of the town. From 1583 et 1813 it belonged to the Capuchins, who again took possession of it in 1850, but it has lately been converted into a naval school. It contains five cloisters, a charming veranda, and magnificent points of view. A spacious grotto to the left in front of the building was formerly used as a Calvary, or series of devotional stations.

POESTUM

No traveller should leave Naples without visiting the antiquity of Paestum. This ancient town was founded by *Greeks from Sybaris* about the year B. C. 600. The ancient name of *Poseidonia* (city of Neptune) sufficient'y indicates its Greek origin. After the conquest of Pyrrhus, Poseidonia fell into the hands of the Romans B. C. 273. who sent a colony thither and changed the name to Poestum. The prosperity of the Greek city was now gone and gradually fell to decay. Christianity took root here at an early period. When the Saracens devasted Paestum in the 9.ᵗᵗ century the inhabitants fled with their bishop to the neighbouring heights, and there founded *Capaccio Vecchio*. Those who appreciate the simple majesty of Greek architecture should endeavour, if possible before quitting Naples to pay a visit to the temples of Paestum. The ancient *Town walls* forming an irregular pentagon, on the river Salso, not far from the coast, about 3 miles in circumference, constructed of blocks of travertine, are almost entirely preserved, outside the latter fragments of an aqueduct pavement of the road, several towers. Most of the object discovered in the course of the excavation which are still continued are preserved in the Museum at Naples. The Temples at Paestum of ancient Greek construction, are the finest extant monuments of this description. They are three in number. The largest and most beautiful is that in the centre the so called. *Temple of Neptune* 66 1[2 yards in length 26 2[3 yards in width, at each extremity are 6 massive, fluted Doric colums 30 feet in height: on each side 12, in all 36 colums of 7 1[2 f. in diameter all well preserved. In the interior of the Cella are two series of 8 colums each (about 6 f. in diameter) with a second row of smaller colums above, which supported the roof. The stone is a species of travertine, The temple was a hypoethron i. e. the cella where the image stood was uncovered; however as its entire character betokens is one of the most ancient specimens of Greek art. To the South of the latter risesthe second temple the so called. *Basilica* (a misnomer) of more recent origin, but also of great antiquity. It is 60 1[2 yards in length 27 y. in width, and its 50 colums are 6 f. in diameter. At each extremity 9 colums on each side 16 also of travertine stone. In front of these temples probably extended the Forum of the ancient town, basements for altars or statues are still recognised here. Near the entrance from Salerno, stands the small *Temple of Ceres* or Vesta with a peristyle of 34 colums, 6 at each end and 11 on either side. Length 36 1[4 yards, width 16 y: colums 5 f. in diameter. This temple too, bears the impress of the simple and majestic Grecian architecture. Between the latter and the Temple of Neptune a few fragments of Roman building have been discovered, a Thea-

3

34

tre, and Amphitheatre it is believed. The latter is
intersected by the road.

To ensure the safety and add to the comfort of
travellers wishing to visit the ruins of Paestum
and the beautiful coast of Amalfi M.ʳ Hugh Darley
has since 1866 made such arrangements with the
Railway company, and the Hotel Keepers of Salerno and Amalfi, as he trusts will fully satisfy the
demand of the travelling public. He undertakes to
conduct a party of not less than sixteen persons
to Amalfi and Paestum and back for frs 50, each
person, which sum will cover all the expense of the
journey, viz. Omnibusses to and from the station,
first class railway and carriage fares; breakfast dinner and lodging at Salerno, luncheon at Amalfi
and Paestum. The party it is proposed shall leave
Naples every Wednesday morning, omnibusses
starting from Vittoria N.° 29 at 7 1[2 a m. They will
first proceed by rail to *Vietri* where carriages will
be in waiting to convey them to *Amalfi* and having
lunched they will proceed to *Salerno* in time for
dinner at 6 p. m. Here they will spend the night
and take an early train on the following morning
after breakfast for *Battipaglia* where they will find
carriages to convey them to *Paestum*. Two hours
will be sufficient to see the Temples and other an-
tiquities, when the excursionists will return to *Battipaglia* in time to meet the last train to Naples.

Every information can be obtained relative to
this excursion and tickets purchased at the office
of Mess.ʳˢ Cerulli C. Bankers N° 29 Vittoria where
names can be registered.

PHARMACY OF THE LYON

DI

LONARDO AND ROMANO

Toledo 303 Naples

Elixir of quinea.

Wine of quinea.

Antigotty Pills.

Chinese drops for bodily stren-
gth Pectoral Lozenges.

Balsam and astringent Inje-
ction.

Sals of quinino from the best English
manufactories

HOTEL AND PENSION

DU

PLEBISCITA

Opposite the Royal Palace

NAPLES

ENTRANCE

Via Gennaro Serra N. 24

Rooms and prices moderate.

Table d'hôte and in the apartment.

Carriage.

All clean and elegantly furnisheed.

View of the bay and Vesuvius.

A LA
CORBEILLE DE FLEURS

J. ZEMPT and SON

HAIR DRESSER AND PERFUMERS

Shampooing and Hair Brushed by Machine

Via S. Caterina a Chiaja, 6

manufacturers of the celabrated

NAPLES SOAP

Strada Arenaccia Foria

LARCE ASSORTMENT OF ENGHISH AND
FRENCH PERFUMERY

ENGHISH FRENCH GERMAN SPOKEN

CROMOLITHOGRAPHY
OF VICTOR STEEGER
Recompensed in different exhibitions
NAPLES
Via Gennaro Serra 22 (Grottone di Palazzo)

Dravings engrassed, in cromolithography, with pencil and pen.

Geographical Mapps.

Commercial executions, antography.

Speciality in etiquetts, cards.

Cardbord, participations of all kind.

Colections of Bacchanals and centaurs . . . L. 10

Planches of Pompel. . . . . » 3

Plans of Naples . . . . » 1

  » » the environs of Naples. . . . . . » 1

  » » Pompel. . . . . » 1

GENNARO BUONO
SURGEON DENTIST

Strada di Chiaia N. 30 first floor

Respectfully announces to have made a set of teeth, which for its shape and materials produces a perfect mastication never before had from any other system both national and foreign, and which he garantees for ten years — He also makes sets in chaoutchou so perfect and natural as to produce no harm to the gums—He wooks also in gold Ippopotamo and any other system required.

CHARLES ANNUNZIATA

JEWELS

Coral—Lava and Tortoiseshell

Manufacturer

Strada S. Carlo, Num. 15.

NAPLES

GENNARO D'AMATO

AND BROTHERS

CORAL MANUFACTORY

Largo S. Croce, Torre del Greco

(with Deploma)

PENSION D'EUROPE

THE NEW PROPRIETOR

M.ʳ GIUSEPPE DELLA CROCE

Has renewed and embellished all the apartments

Facing the south and west

STRADA S. TERESA A CHIAIA N. 10

NAPLES

Hotel della Bella Venezia

KEPT BY

GUSTAVO TRAPP

Situated in the center of the City

Via Carminello Toledo N. 1

NAPLES

Rooms from L. 1.50 to L. 5 per day

Dinner at a moderate prices

CARMINE GRASSI

HAIR DRESSER FOR LADIES AND GENTLEMEN

Deposit of foreign

AND NATIONAL PERFUMERY

Strada Pace a Chiaia N. 29

NAPLES

ARTISTS STUDIOS

CAV. TOMMASO DE VIVO

and FRANCESCO TROTTA

PAINTERS

Orders received in every sort of art
Exportation

Depôt of old pictures

Ex Couvent of S. Maria la Nuova — NAPLES

EXCURSION TRIP

TO AMALFI and PAESTUM

BY M.ʳ HUGH DARLEY

OF NAPLES

Price — **Fs. 50** all encluded

Apply to Messieurs **CERULLI et C.**

29 Vittoria

SORRENTO GOODS

GARGIULO AND PISCICELLI

Deposit of Sorrento works

, and glove manufactory

~~~~~~~~~~~

Calata S. Caterina a Chiaia N. 44

NAPLES

THE GOLDEN LION

A variety of pantaloons, cravats, collars, wrists
English and French perfumery

And other articles at reduced prices

Toledo 422 — NAPLES

HAT WAREHOUSE
LAROSSA ET SON

foreign and national
HATS MANUFACTURER

STRADA TOLEDO N. 58

NAPLES

ORIENTAL HOUSE
REPT BY **CLEOMÈNES DUZOVITZ**

OF CONSTANTINOPLES

Large collection of Turkish Indian Chinese
and Japonese curiosities

Foreign orders received

Strada di Chiaia N. 78.

SEWING MACHINES

From **Wheeler** and **Wilson** factory Americans;
guaranteed for their perfection in sewing, slight
motion, and quantity of accessories.

ORDERS RECEIVED

PAOLA SANTINI — Toledo 186 — *Naples*

LABORATORY

Works in coloured marbles from **Cave Izzo** in **Vitulano**

Directed by **RAIMONDO BELLIAZZI**

Piazza Cavour N. 31 and 32 — NAPLES

Foreign orders received

LOUIS STRAJANO

HAIR DRESSER

DEPOSIT OF GOOD PERFUMERY

Strada di Chiala N. 66, first floor

Naples

Permanent Exhibition

FOR OBJECTS OF FINE ARTS TO SELL

and Photograph Etablishment Rept by G. ARENA

Entrance by the garden in Piazza dei Martiri

and N. 7 Strada Pace — NAPLES

GARBERO PANTALEONE

UPHOLSTERER AND MATTRES MAKER

Strada Monteoliveto N. 56

NAPLES

GENNARO DE ANGELIS

Coral, lava and Tortoiseshell merchant

Strada S. Carlo N. 29

NAPLES

SOAP MANUFACTORY

FELICE GENEVOIS ET SON

perfumers

and manufacturers of Naples soap to the greatest porfection

Sold at the *Abeille d'Or* Toledo 92
And wholesale at vico Salato all' Olivello n. 30
and at the Marchet place N. 96 et 97

NAPLES

CHEESE WARCHOUSE

SAUSAGES, CHEESE, WINES LIQUORS

BY G. PAUTASSO

SUCCESSOR OF **CIRIO** ET **COMP.**°

N. 54, Largo Palazzo — **NAPLES**

GENNARO BIANCONCINI

Book binder and setter of all sorts of broidcries

STATIONERY

PHOTOGRAPHS FIGURS

Prayer books and gilt frames

Rue di Chiaia N. 57 — NAPLES

Large Laboratory
O. FORTI et C.°

Leather and cloth articles, a spochet-books Purses, Travelling bags, Inkstand, portrat-frames ec. at cost price.

Strada di Chiaia N. 51

NAPLES

GIOVANNI SANGES
HAIR DRESSER FOR LADIES AND GENTLEMEN

Deposit of foreign perfumery

Vico Baglivo Uries N. 36

NAPLES

Restaurant de Strasburgh
REPT DY

GIOVANNI SCOTTI
Vico due Porte a Toledo N. 45

Dinners served ont, and orders received, French English and German cooking.

THE NEW LIBRARY

ENGLISH, ITALIAN, FRENCH AND GERMAN BOOK

Orders, and deposit—Subscriptions to Newspapers

Strada Toledo N. 140

NAPLES

MERLINO
CORAL, CAMEOS, AND LAVA WAREHOUSE
Strada Gigante N. 18 e 19
Naples

GALLERY OF PAITINGS
SCULPTURES, BRONZES AND ALABASTERS
Rept by Artist **G. MORMILE**
Rivès photographs, Great collection of the best
artists in guash
38, Chiatamone opposite the Castle dell' Uovo

Collection of ancient articles
PASQUALE IANNIELLO
Strada Costantinopoli N. 92 e 93
Deposit in the same street N. 26 1.ª floor
NAPLES

PRIMA DIGESTIO FIT IN ORE
Immediate and sure recovery from tooth-ache
and all other disease of the mouth by Professor
Bisaccia, Physician and Surgeon Dentist appro-
ved by the Royal University of Naples.

Teeth and artificial sets.
Strada Chiaia N. 229 — NAPLES

LUIGI OTTAJANO

WOOD CARVER

Honorary Professor to the Royal School of fine
Art in Naples

Teacher in Ornaments at the Drawing school
of the Working class

Silver Medal at the London Exhibition of 1872
and Deploma at Vienna in 1873

NAPLES — Rue Constantinoples N. 27

D. A. Sarmientos

Surgeon Dentist

It is warmly recommented by Doctor Sarmientos for
the benefit of the public in general never to forget that ex-
tracting the teeth is not curing them but a mutilation un-
worthy in our days—No tooth ache has ever been repea-
ted by those who have carefully followed the cure which
M.' Sarmientos has acquired in ten years practice — He
makes new sets of artificial teeth by a new system in order
to fit well the most sensible and delicate mouth. garen-
teing the mastication.

His house in open from 9 a. m. to 5 p. m.

Strada di Chiaia N. 238 Palazzo Nethery

NAPLES

GRAN BEER HOUSE
Toledo 292 — NAPLES

VIENNA BEER

the only deposit in this town

Restorant at fixed price and a la carte — Foreign and country wines — Large rooms with billiards and other games.

PENSION

REPT BY **GIOVANNI CENCI**
Strada S. Brigida N. 48 — NAPLES

Rooms good dinner and breakfast L. 5 per day
Furnished rooms from 2 to 5 franks per day
Situated in the most central part of the town

HYDROTERAPIC ESTABLISHMENT

DIRECTED BY **Dott. M. Guariglia**

Idroterapic cure. Fresh sea and mineral baths. Russian baths and stoves. The Establishment is open from 7 a. m. to 7 p. m.
Via Carlo Doria — Salita Museo — NAPLES

ARTIFICIAL TEETH
IMMUTABLE AND IMPROVED
under te American systeme

BY PROFESSOR **G. CAMMAROTA** SURGEON DENTIST
Tooth ache cured in one time, and any operation of the teeth done by the superiority of his sistem.
Strada S. Carlo N. 16 — NAPLES
near Kernot's pharmary

Hôtel d'Angleterre

SALERNO

Kept by the Widow **SALVI**

Finely situated. Large and small apartments

English and French spoken

Hotel Gran Bretagne

VILLA CIOFFI CASTAGNETO

CAVA

Table d'hôte, Board and lodging, pension,
at a moderate price

Garden and terrace on the south looking the sea

LOUIS LABRIOLA

TORTOISE SHELL MERCHANT

Strada Chiatamone N. 23 ground floor

Naples

Antiquity Warehouse

Ancient furniture, pictures, guash, and fine arts

Strada Pace — Palace Nunsiante N. 11 to 15

NAPLES

RAFFAELE, LEOPOLDO AND NICOLA MANZIONE

Execute all sorts of private and public

MARBLE WORKS

FOREIGN ORDERS

Place Cavour N. CC, Naples

PENSION ANGLO SWISS

Villa Sorrentino Belvedere at Cava S. Pietro

REPT BY MISS GOTTREAUX

Finely situated both for winter and summer — Surrounded by beautiful landscapes, and offers fine promenade, and drive.

Moderate prices — CAVA

JOHN STELLA

ENGRAVER ON CAMEOS

LAVA, TORTOISESHELL AND CORAL

ORDERS RECEIVED FOR EXPORTATION

....

LIKENESS TAKEN TO PERFECTION

Medals from the Dublin exhibition 1865 and Naples 1871

Strada Pace N. 9

NAPLES

LARGE RIDING SCHOOL

DIRECTED BY

M.ʳ JOSEPH CAROPRESO

Vico Cupa Riviera di Chiaja

NAPLES

Private hortes and for sale are received, Deposit of
Sadlery, Riding lessons for ladies and gentlemen
both by day and evening, Horses let for the promenade, subscriptions and pension ee made according the tarif and rules of the establishment.

www.ingramcontent.com/pod-product-compliance
Lightning Source LLC
Chambersburg PA
CBHW030721110426
42739CB00030B/1074